Boutique Business
A Guide for Budding Entrepreneurs
Who Can't Find Answers on Google

Jance Chartae

DEDICATION

This book is dedicated to all the retail managers that molded me to become the professional that I am today and all of the customers that I met along the way.

I also want to dedicate this book to the countless women with dreams of owning a boutique, but who felt like they couldn't do it alone. For a while it may have felt impossible. It may have felt like there were no answers out there to all of your questions. But, the answers are out there! The issue is that there aren't alot of women willing to help other women to find success in this industry. It is my goal to help as much as I can and to share all of the knowledge I have. I sincerely hope and pray that you all find success.

I have to thank my YouTube subscribers. Because of their countless questions, I felt compelled to provide answers.

Last, but certainly not least, I want to dedicate this book to my loving husband who egged me on every single day, pushed me to try new things and think in new ways; who believed in me when I lacked belief in myself and told me he was proud of me countless times a day. For that, I love and thank you.

CONTENTS

1 INTRODUCTION

"I want to open a boutique… but I don't know where to start."

This is currently the mindstate of many women across the world. I, like these women, have been in that place before. I'd worked in retail for ten years and I was tired of clocking in and out. I was tired of working for someone else. I was ready to take my career to the next level.

So, what did I do? Probably the same thing that many of you did. I picked up my phone, opened the Google app and typed "How to Open a Boutique." And what did I learn? Basically, nothing. So, I went to my second favorite search engine, YouTube! And what did I find there? A bunch of women claiming to be "successful" boutique owners, but not providing very helpful information.

Strangely, it seemed that boutique owners were being very "hush, hush" about the industry and how they had found this so-called "success." I was shocked that there was not one video or article out there that gave me a good description of how to start a business. I was lost…

Fast forward to 2016. An opportunity literally fell into my lap! I accepted a job as the store manager of a small boutique in St. Louis, MO where I was able to build a store to be whatever I wanted it to be. Literally, it was like it was my store. My direct boss had ZERO retail experience and told me that I was basically on my own.

Not only was I allowed to buy wholesale merchandise to sell at the shop, the best part was that I was spending someone else's money. There was absolutely no risk involved for me. It was truly a blessing.

But, I knew that my goal was to one day own my own boutique. So, I took this job as an opportunity to make as many mistakes as possible on someone else's dime. I didn't purposely make mistakes, but I looked at this as strictly a learning opportunity. I felt that if I could help this shop to find success then I would have no problem owning my own shop one day.

It is now 2018 and I will proudly proclaim that I am an amazing buyer. It brings me such joy when customers compliment the collections that come into the store each month. I love to hear a customer say, "My friends always ask me where I get my clothes and I send them here" or "I never find anything at the mall that I like, but I always find something here." I love to hear customers ask "When is the next collection coming?" These are literally my proudest moments at work.

Now, I will be honest. Every day is not amazing. There are days when we don't make as much money or see as many customers. There are times when I purchase an item to sell at the shop and it doesn't resonate well so I have to find a way to sell it. At times I price things too high or wish I had prices something higher. There are no perfect days when running a boutique. But, it is so much fun and more importantly it is rewarding.

I will be the first to admit that running a boutique is not a smooth operation. Whether you have a brick and mortar location or an online boutique, you will have your struggles. But, I promise there is light at the end of the tunnel. I am here to show you the light. Take my hand as I lead you in the right direction.

Now as a disclaimer, I want to tell you that I do NOT consider myself to be an expert, but I DO consider myself to be a professional, an amazing salesperson, an awesome store manager, a successful retail buyer and a beast at providing customer service and memorable store experiences. So, with that being said, please know that I do not claim to have all of the right answers, but I know a lot and I am willing to share it! That's it, that's all.

OK, now let's go back to YouTube for a second, because that it how this all started and how the idea of this book came along.

There is a young lady on YouTube who's name I will not mention, but I have a feeling that you all have probably seen her videos before. While watching one of her videos I was completely taken aback by some of her statements. She said, "One of my pet peeves is when somebody has the audacity to ask me where I get my product from... I find that to be an insult. It is an insult because, why do you see it fair for us to just hand you our resources and lay them all on the table for you...?"

* inserts shocked emoji *

* pauses video *

It all made sense now. After days of Googling and researching I realized that I couldn't find the information I needed because no one was willing to share it.

GASP

* back to the video *

She goes on to say, "I will never share that with you, so please respectfully do not ask me."

My reaction: "Girl bye! It isn't that serious!" I couldn't believe it. These women were out here finding success and didn't want to "make it too easy" for the next woman. These women were literally holding out on information because they felt that because they had struggled, everyone else should struggle as well. The competition and selfishness is real out here.

We grew up being told things like "there is no such thing as a dumb question" and "you'll never know unless you ask." And here we are asking questions, yet getting no answers. People are literally not willing to help.

And at that very moment it became my goal to share every ounce of knowledge that I have. From where I get our merchandise, to how much we pay for it, to how much we price it at, and so much more; here I am about to throw all these resources at you like confetti!

So, are you ready to learn the basics of buying merchandise for your boutique? I know you are! Well, put on your tallest high heels (or strap up your Nike's) and walk on over to the next page.

2 ARE YOU READY

If you've made it to this page, congratulations! You're well on your way to having a successful boutique of your own. By purchasing this book you have indicated that you are ready to invest in yourself. I want to tell you that I am proud of you!

So, let me begin by saying that it is very important that you are legally ready to open a boutique and have acquired all of the required licensing. Whether you intend to have an online boutique or a brick & mortar location, there are a variety of licenses that may be required. Requirements will differ depending on the state, city and/or county you are opening the boutique in. Unfortunately, this is not the book that will tell you how to obtain licensing, but fear not. That book is in the works!

This book, however, will provide you with a few very simple and essential tips for creating a vision for your boutique, as well as purchasing merchandise for your boutique.

Note that you will be required to have an EIN (Employer Identification Number) and/or a Seller's Permit in order to purchase wholesale merchandise whether online or in-person. I know some of you may not have obtained those things yet. DO NOT PANIC! They are easy to get. The hardest part will be choosing your business name. Registering the business name and obtaining the licenses is typically the easy part.

The quickest direction I can give you would be to call your Secretary of State office and inquire about obtaining a business license. Tell them what type of business you intend to open and any other relevant information. I promise they will be able to give you all of the information that you need.

So, now that you've gotten your business license and/or seller's permit, you have your foot in the door. Actually, I'd say your entire body is standing in the doorway and now you just need to step forward. You are more ready than you may think you are. It is now your time to shine!

More than likely, you had a vision for your boutique long before you actually had your license or money to invest in your business. If you do not have a vision, do me a favor and pause right here! PAUSE! Walk away from this book momentarily, grab a pen and paper, and start brainstorming what your vision is.

You would be doing yourself a HUGE disservice if you opened a boutique (or any business for that matter) while lacking a vision. As you brainstorm, don't think small-scale or short-term. Take this vision as far as you possibly can. Not only should you be thinking about what you want to sell, but also how much you want to sell it for. When thinking about how much you want to sell merchandise for, you should also think about how much you want to spend on merchandise.

Do you only want to sell online? Do you want to open one boutique? Do you want to open multiple boutiques across the country one day? Do you want all of your items to cost less than $30? How much are you willing to pay to rent your retail space? Do you want new styles coming in weekly, bi-weekly, monthly?... There are so many things to think about.

OK, are you back now? Good! I'm happy that you have created a vision. Remember that you can change your mind. You can add to this vision or take something away at any time. However, it is very valuable to have a vision when you first start your business. Think of it as a blueprint or a guide book. I promise that it will help you.

So, now you are ready to make your first purchase!

There are various ways that you can go about purchasing merchandise for your boutique. There are various places that you can purchase merchandise from. In this book I will share three of the best ways to acquire the best merchandise for your boutique.

OK, ladies! It's go-time!

3 HOW TO SELECT MERCHANDISE

Selecting the right merchandise for your boutique is the most important step after obtaining your business licensing. There are thousands, if not millions, of styles to choose from on this earth.

When selecting your merchandise, you may be thinking it's most important to sell something that no one else is selling. But, to be honest, you can sell all the same things as another store on your block as long as you're selling it a different way. Now, this is a topic for another book, but this is what I'm trying to say...

You should sell something that no one else is offering in your area, but this may not be your merchandise. It might be an experience. Let me give you an example; probably not the best example, but here it is... Yesterday I was in Rainbow, a store that I honestly do not care for, but I saw something nice from the window. I spotted a jumpsuit that I loved. It cost $16.97. Then I went next door, literally next door, to Charlotte Russe and they were selling the exact same jumpsuit, in the exact same color for $4 more. No joke. It was literally the exact same jumpsuit from the exact same vendor.

The interesting thing about this is that many people don't know or realize that many of the stores in this world buy their merchandise from the same vendors. Sometimes we'd never know because 1) they change the label on the item to reflect their company name and 2) we don't shop at every single store.

I don't typically shop at Rainbow for various reasons. I don't typically care for the customer service that is provided, or lack thereof. I don't care for their marketing or the atmosphere of the store, and the quality of many of their items isn't the greatest.

Yet, there's a store right next door, Charlotte Russe, selling multiple items that Rainbow is selling. Crazy, right? Yes, they are both younger, female brands, but because they offer two different store experiences most people wouldn't know that they carry some of the same items. We wouldn't know that the quality of many of their items is exactly the same. We don't realize that we could be saving a dollar or two at the store right next door because we don't care for the brand, the message, the atmosphere... the overall store experience is not pleasing to us. Even more interesting is some people don't care to save the money simply because they don't care to support certain brands.

I say all this to say that the experience that you offer can mean a lot more than the product that you're selling. But, again, that's another book...

What is your company going to stand for? What type of experience will you provide that will set you apart from the rest? Once you figure those things out you can sell almost anything!

While you ponder on that, let's talk about actually selecting merchandise. Please know that your boutique does not have to cover all categories. Your boutique could sell just clothing or just shoes, etc. You can sell whatever you'd like and as much as you'd like.

4 THE PAY METHOD

One of the most important steps that you should take before you buy any merchandise is to do your research. Your research will involve the use of something I like to call "*The Pay Method.*"

Now, *The Pay Method* doesn't involve actual payment with money for anything. Instead you will pay a visit to other shops. You will pay attention to what they sell. You will pay attention to how they service their customers, etc. You get what you PAY for. So, if you don't PAY attention and if you don't do your research then you'll end up paying the price for sure and that might include a hefty amount of failure and wasted money.

So, here is what you should do! Shop the competition (and shop it often)! Check out their product assortment. Study their sell-through. How much has been sold or been marked down since the last time you were there? Are their shoes selling or does it look like they're struggling to sell them? What appears to be selling? What are shoppers carrying around in their hands?

Ask as many questions as possible without looking like you're casing the place. Let them know if it's your first time in the boutique. Ask them what their best seller is currently or what their favorite item in the store is. Pay attention to how they provide customer service. Pay attention to how the customers interact or if they interact at all. Pay attention to how many people leave the store with a shopping bag versus leaving empty-handed.

Here is the most important tip! You need to try on their clothing. Grab as much of their merchandise as you can and take it into the fitting room. Even if you don't actually like the items, take them into the fitting room. While you're in the fitting room pay attention to the brand names. If you're in a local boutique more than likely their clothing will still have the original vendors name on the label. Take out your phone and take photos. Create a list. Record the names of the brands. Take notes about how they fit, how they feel. How is the quality? Good or bad? How are they priced? Take as many notes as you possibly can.

Larger stores like Charlotte Russe, Forever 21, Rainbow, and even stores like Macy's can be great sources for research. In recent months I've noticed that a lot of Charlotte Russe's clothing do not reflect the brand's name and instead still has the name of the vendor they purchased the item from.

Repeat the steps above. Visit other stores. Try on their merchandise. Take notes. Anything that looks even remotely interesting to you or if the quality looks amazing, write it down!

You'll be shocked to know that you, as a small business owner, can carry the exact same clothing brands as many large retailers. On multiple occasions in the last month I have found items being sold at Charlotte Russe that I had purchased months before for my job. Initially it blew my mind. Now, it's rewarding! It's validating! It lets me know that any of us are capable of selling whatever we want.

I hope that was motivating for you.

OK, now that you've done some research, let's talk about the different ways that you can purchase merchandise for your boutique. But, before we proceed, **remember your product will not sustain your business; your attitude, your customer service and your overall store experience will.**

5 L.A. FASHION DISTRICT

My first in-person buying experience took place in the L.A. Fashion District. How would I describe it, you ask? Imagine an outdoor shopping experience that covers 90 blocks. That is the L.A. Fashion District.

The Fashion District is described as the mecca of the apparel industry. 70% of the Fashion District is estimated to be wholesale-related business. Looking for textiles? You'll find the largest selection here as well. If you own a boutique or are planning to open a boutique, wholesale vendors are what you're looking for.

For more information about the Fashion District visit fashiondistrict.org. Scroll to the bottom of the page, select "wholesale directory" and search for what you're looking for. You can even see where each shop is located on the map.

Shopping the Fashion District is my favorite way to shop for wholesale merchandise. I enjoy being able to touch and feel the merchandise before purchasing it. I enjoy being able to talk to a live human being in-person and I definitely enjoy being able to take my merchandise home with me. I mean let's be honest, who really enjoys buying something online and having to wait 5-7 business days for it to be delivered? Answer: no one!

I do most of my buying in the San Pedro Wholesale Mart. You can learn more about this division of the Fashion District at sanpedromart.com. The website is pretty basic, but once there you can search for vendors by name or by category which is super easy.

Some of my favorite vendors in San Pedro include Double Zero, FAVLUX, Iris, Les Amis and Zenana to name a few.

Before you visit the Fashion District, there are a few guidelines that can help you to have a seamless and successful buying trip.

My golden rule is to PLAN! I'm sure you remember the saying "if you fail to plan, then you plan to fail." That definitely applies here. You do NOT want to be walking aimlessly through 90 blocks of stores like a chicken with its head cut off. Do yourself a favor and refer to the map. Before you go, decide what you're looking for and start there. Then work your way from store to store.

Whenever I go on a buying trip I like to create a vision board for what I am looking for. I do this using the Pinterest app on my phone. I typically create a board and title it for whichever season I'm shopping for. Then I add things to the board as inspiration for what to buy. I may add colors that I like or styles of clothing that I find appealing; anything that will give me a reference of what to look for when I get there.

When you arrive in the Fashion District it is very important that you remember that you are shopping for your boutique and not for your closet. It does not matter if your boutique is named after you. Do not fill your boutique with a bunch of items that would only be suitable and appealing to you and your body type. Shop for other people's body types, not just your own. It's always nice to have a good variety of styles for customers to choose from. I have purchased many items for our shop that I would never actually wear myself, but I knew would be appealing to another audience.

6 ADVANTAGES OF PURCHASING MERCHANDISE IN-PERSON

There is definitely advantages to purchasing merchandise in-person rather than online. Not only do you get to see and feel the merchandise before buying, you also have the chance to build a relationship with a live human being who works in a shop. Your interaction with that worker can be very important. It could mean the difference in you paying $9 for an item or $10.50 for an item. Yes, I am telling you that it's possible for you to negotiate prices. It doesn't always happen. But it's much easier to do when you're standing right in front of the person and they want to make a sale.

I typically begin my negotiation tactics by telling the worker how in love with the item(s) I am. I walk around the store with them in my hands and this makes the worker excited because just like any other store these people have goals to make and they are determined to make a sale.

After I've made all of my selections I take them up to the counter or to the worker so that we can start totaling the order and talking prices. Once they've told me my total, I typically let them know that I've went over my budget... even if I have not actually gone over my budget.

At this point the worker may be caught off guard because they thought they were about to make a huge sale. So, I start picking up each item, one-by-one and asking about the prices. If something is $8, I may ask if they can do $7. They may say no. So then I ask if they can do $7.50. They might say no again. So then I ask if they can do $7.75 and they agree. You never know what they may agree to. But, remember you need to make money and so do they. More than likely they just want you to take the merchandise home so there's probably some wiggle room for negotiation if it will result in a definite sale.

If you feel comfortable, you can do that with every single item in your order. The worst that could happen is they may say "no" and guess what you're going to do? Move on to the next item. I know it may not seem like saving .25 cents is a lot, but remember that you are paying by the item. All of those cents can add up to big dollars saved at the end of the day. So, save where you can.

After you've made your purchase they may have the items on-hand or they might need to call their warehouse to have it packaged and sent over to them. Either way it does not matter. Ask them if they can hold the merchandise while you continue to shop. You want to keep your hands as free as possible. But, it's very important that you keep track of what you've purchased. Leave a business card with them, take one of theirs, make sure you get a receipt/invoice and make sure you keep a record of where they're located. Now, on to the next shop!

Another important tip is to ask for help. If you can't find something, ask for help. On one of my buying trips I was searching high and low for plus-size merchandise. I couldn't find it anywhere!

After a while I finally stopped and asked one of the store owners if they knew where I might be able to find some. To my surprise they told me exactly what street to visit. If I had opened my mouth and asked earlier though, I could've saved a lot of time.

Lastly, as mentioned above, I love being able to take the merchandise I purchased home with me. So, my last tip is to be sure to bring empty luggage.

Alright, so before we move on to the next chapter, here's a brief recap and a few essential tips to help you survive your L.A. Fashion District trip.

- Save time by using a map and asking for directions.
- Save money by negotiating prices.
- Save your arm strength by leaving bags with the vendor after purchasing.
- Save space in your luggage by having larger items shipped.
- Save space in your luggage by only packing lightweight and small items that you purchased.
- Save your feet by wearing comfy shoes.
- Save more money by parking in a parking garage rather than on the street at a meter.
- Save yourself a headache by shopping early in the week rather than later in the week when it's busier. Ready to explore another wholesale buying avenue? Well, let's move on.

7 FASHIONGO.NET

Have you ever purchased an outfit online from a company that you'd never purchased from and then when you received the item it didn't look anything like you thought it would, nor did it fit well?

Well imagine buying hundreds of items from multiple stores that you've never heard of, half of them not looking anything like you thought they would and not being able to return them for a refund… Welcome to the world of online shopping for wholesale buyers. Sounds frightening doesn't it? Well, welcome to fashiongo.net.

FashionGo has honestly been one of the greatest resources for me as a buyer. Because there are so many vendors selling their merchandise on the site it has allowed me to browse through thousands of items at one time all at the click of a button. I've been able to compare prices and even find multiple vendors selling the exact same items for different prices. The only drawback to purchasing online is simply that you don't know exactly what you're getting until it arrives. Unless you're familiar with the quality of that company's merchandise, you may be in for a total surprise when your items arrive.

Before I say too much I have to mention that you must register for an account in order to gain access to fashiongo.net. The good news is that getting a buyer membership is completely free, it's quick and easy. The initial application asks for your seller's permit, but don't panic if you have not acquired one yet. Our shop was able to gain access to the site by submitting the following documents;

- Copy of approved application for EIN
- Certificate of Organization from our state

The site may also ask for two recent invoices/receipts.

FashionGo also provides access to international buyers as well. International buyers will be required to submit two recent invoices/receipts from wholesale apparel/fashion-related vendors. A business license or seller's permit is not required for buyers outside the United States.

My first buying experience took place on fashiongo.net. Since I'm being completely honest with you, I'm going to say it was a little nerve wrecking. I had NEVER purchased anything at a wholesale value, not to mention spent over $1,000 on anything. Every purchase seemed like a huge risk being taken. To be completely honest, there's a lot of risks involved.

You don't know if your items will look the same in person, you don't know how it fits, if the color is actually what you think it is, if it stretches, if one of the items in the pack will be damaged... There are literally so many things to worry about. But, again I'm here to help. If I can eliminate a risk or two for you all then that's what I'm going to do. If I can help a boutique owner save a few dollars then that's what I'm going to do.

OK, so you've just gotten approved for an account on FashionGo and you have no idea what to do next, right? Just start scrolling! This is the easiest and fastest way to become familiar with the website and to see what product is available.

If you know the type of merchandise you are looking for then don't waste your time searching through other types of items. For instance, if you know you're going to be selling women's clothing then don't waste time browsing through the men's assortment. If you know you're not going to sell accessories, then don't waste time looking at them. It is very important that you stay focused because it is super easy to become 1) overwhelmed and 2) distracted while shopping on FashionGo.

So, typically after you log into your account on FashionGo you will be brought to the homepage. On this page you will see a variety of featured vendors and items of the day. As you continue to scroll you will see a section called "Vendor Spotlight," a section called "Recommended for You" (which may be empty if you are a new user), then "New Vendors" and lastly "Today's New Items." Note that the listings on the homepage change daily so check back regularly to see what's new.

I always like to start from the top and work my way down the screen. The vendors/items listed at the top of the page are typically new and fresh items from popular vendors. These vendors typically have very good ratings and are overall very credible. Think of it this way. The best and most credible vendors are at the top of the page and the newbies who haven't proved themselves yet are at the bottom.

Now, take a moment to click on everything! I mean everything! Start from the first vendor you see, click on it and browse through their collection. Then return to the home page, click on the next vendor and repeat. Click on everything on the homepage.

Done? Great! Now you're familiar with six vendors available on FashionGo. Spoiler alert! There are way more than six vendors available on FashionGo... so brace yourself! Now that you've looked through the homepage it's time to dig deeper.

Next we'll discuss the different ways that you can search for items on FashionGo.

8 FASHIONGO.NET – SEARCH BAR

Using the search bar on FashionGo can be very helpful. Below are the different ways that you can search.

- By category (Select from women, shoes, accessories, handbags, men, children, other)
- By style number
- By vendor

In the search bar you can type anything and the results will show relevant items to whatever you typed. For example, type the phrase "leather mini skirt." As you're typing you will see things pop up in the drop down menu below the search bar. You can then select from "product in category" or "all products" that may match the description of what you're looking for . Another option is that you can just click the search icon and see what pops up. For this example, we are just going to click the search icon (or "enter") and see what pops up.

You'll likely see a variety of items pop up on the screen. As you scroll you'll notice that they are all different colors and lengths. Beneath each photo is the name of the vendor, as well as the price that they are selling the item for.

Do you see an item you like, but you aren't quite ready to purchase it or add it to your cart? Hover over the photo of the item you like with your mouse and you will see three small icons pop up at the bottom of the photo. Select the "heart" icon and this item will be added to your "favorites." You can add as many items as you like to your "favorites". You can even add a vendor to your favorites, which we will get too soon.

So, as you continue to scroll you may start to notice duplicates of items that you've already seen. Surprise! There are multiple vendors selling the exact same items; sometimes for the same price and sometimes for a higher or lower price. If you've already favorited an item and you see it again for a cheaper price, favorite that one too. Also, sometimes items may be sold out by the time you're ready to move an item from your favorites to your cart. It can help, though, if you're familiar with three other vendors selling the exact same item.

A side note: You may also notice that different vendors may even use the same photos of a model wearing a particular style. I think it's quite hilarious.

OK, back to business. Did you find a vendor that you're in love with? You can favorite the entire shop. While on a vendor's homepage you'll see a bar that says "favorite store" at the top of the screen. Click it! You have now added this shop to your list of favorite vendors.

Another great tip for using the search bar to find very specific items is to **sort** the styles. If you're anything like me when shopping online, you like to view items from lowest price to highest price. Guess what? You can do this on FashionGo too. It's truly a blessing and saves me the burden of having to look through hundreds of items that are out of our price range.

9 FASHIONGO.NET – THE MENU

Using the menu at the top of the page you can search by a variety of categories. Below is a list of the categories available on FashionGo.

- Vendors
  - By alphabet
  - By category (women's, men's, etc.)
  - New Vendors
  - Promotions
  - Featured Vendor
  - Drop down menu of all vendors in alphabetical order
- New arrivals
  - Arrivals by date
  - Arrivals by category
- Women
  - By style; each with more specific options listed underneath
  - Tops
  - Dresses
  - Jackets/Outerwear
  - Pants
  - Skirts
  - Denim
  - Party Dresses
  - Sets
  - Swimwear
  - Lingerie & Hosiery
  - Featured Shops

- Plus-size
- Juniors
- Missy
- Young Contemporary
- Maternity
- Shoes
  o By Category (boots, booties, dress shoes, flats heels, etc.)
- Accessories
  o By category (sunglasses, scarves, earrings, necklaces, etc.)
- Handbags
  o By style (backpack, crossbody, messenger, shoulder bag, etc.)
- Men
  o By style (casual shirts, dress shirts, denim, jackets/outerwear, etc.) -
- Kids
  o Boys
  o Girls
  o Infants
- More -
  o Cosmetics
  o Fixtures/Displays
  o Keychains
  o Perfumes
  o Pets
  o Tech Accessories
  o Other Products

Overall, FashionGo is an amazing resource for new buyers. However, there are risks involved when ordering from vendors that you have neither heard of nor shopped with previously. So, be careful and also be smart. Do your research. After you've found a vendor that you like, Google to see if you can find companies who carry that company's merchandise.

For example, a company called Reborn J sells really beautiful floral dresses. In the Google search bar I typed "Reborn J dress" and then scrolled to see how many stores/boutiques carry they're merchandise. It is especially helpful if you see credible companies displaying merchandise from those vendors.

There are definitely ways that you can eliminate some of the risks of buying wholesale. Below are a few tips that will be helpful when ordering wholesale merchandise online.

1.   Have a plan. Know what you're looking for… styles, colors, price, etc. Stay focused and don't get distracted by all the other pretty things until you find the item(s) you're looking for.
2.   Use the search bar to search for the exact type of item you're looking for or something similar. Scroll until you find something that satisfies your need.
3.   Favorite many different items. Don't get stuck on ONE particular item.
4.   Send messages or emails to vendors if you are unsure about anything. For example: If you're unsure about the color of the item on the screen ask if it's possible to have a photo emailed to you. Or; if you have a UPS account and would like the shipping of your ordered charged to that account, send an email to the vendor to place the order and make your shipping request.
5.   Read reviews and check ratings for individual vendors.

6. Place pre-orders. The order won't be charged to your account until the items are actually in stock. It also gives you time to change your mind if you find something better or that you like more.

Now before you log off of FashionGo, scroll down to the very bottom of the screen. In the footer section you'll see another menu full of options. Under the section "Our Company" select "Show Info."

On this screen you will see a list of upcoming fashion trade shows in various cities across the U.S. as well as a brief description of each show. It's time to dive into another way to purchase wholesale merchandise for your boutique; attending a fashion trade show.

10 FASHION TRADE SHOWS

Attending a fashion trade show can be amazing or the most overwhelming buying experience depending on which one you attend. For the purposes of this book we're going to focus on MAGIC, the biggest and best of all fashion trade shows.

My first MAGIC trip was just as I described it above; definitely overwhelming, but super amazing! I learned so much valuable information about buying and also all aspects of operating a successful boutique.

MAGIC is described as "the preeminent trade event in the international fashion industry, hosting global buyers and sellers of men's, women's and children's apparel, footwear, accessories and sourcing resources." This trade show takes place twice a year (February and August) in Las Vegas.

If you can attend a fashion trade show in a city near you I'd definitely encourage you to do so, but if you had to choose between all of the trade shows occurring each year, MAGIC would be the one to attend.

11 WHICH SHOW IS FOR YOU?

There are several other shows that take place under the umbrella of MAGIC. There may be more than one that will suit your needs. Below are all of the shows that you can attend at MAGIC;

FN PLATFORM

- FN PLATFORM is a showcase of international, branded footwear. It features footwear brands from more than 30 countries and displays options for men, women, and also children.

WWDMAGIC

- WWDMAGIC features the largest and most comprehensive selection of women's apparel and accessories. Here you can shop on-trend styles for both women and junior's, as well as collections from emerging designers.

THE TENTS

- THE TENTS presents a more elevated shopping experience featuring luxury and designer brands for men, as well as dual-gender styles.

PROJECT

- PROJECT is an amazing showcase of men's contemporary, premium denim and designer collections. Here, one can also find sportswear, accessories and footwear.

PROJECT WOMEN'S

- PROJECT WOMEN'S features more established and well-known brands. At this show, one can find contemporary brands, premium denim, as well as accessories.

STITCH @ PROJECT WOMEN'S

- STITCH showcases an amazing mix of luxury to lifestyle ready-to-wear brands. This show features both domestic and international brands.

THE COLLECTIVE

- THE COLLECTIVE is located next to PROJECT and offers shoppers access to the rapidly growing men's fashion market. This show features branded and licensed apparel for men and young men.

POOLTRADESHOW

- POOLTRADESHOW is the place to be for buyers seeking new and fresh vendors. Brands being sold here are considered to be "emerging" in the boutique industry. At this show you can also find accessories, lifestyle, home goods and stationary. There are also some vendors here that allow "cash & carry."

Curve Las Vegas

- Buyers seeking swimwear and lingerie should definitely attend CURVE LAS VEGAS.

Children's Club

- CHILDREN'S CLUB is the only show in Vegas solely focused on children's contemporary product. The quality of merchandise at this show mirrors that of the contemporary women's options at other shows.

Sourcing at MAGIC

- SOURCING at MAGIC is one's connection to the entire global supply chain. SOURCING at MAGIC allows buyers to discover emerging technology, trending patterns and materials from more than 40 countries across the world.

Footwear Sourcing at MAGIC

- FOOTWEAR SOURCING AT MAGIC allows retailers to work directly with factories across the world in order to source footwear production for their brands. Anyone interested in footwear manufacturing should attend this show.

MAGIC also takes place in Japan each year. MAGIC Japan "connects women's, men's and children's contemporary apparel, footwear, and accessory brands, as well as sourcing suppliers, to the leading retail buyers in Japan, Asia, and around the globe. To learn more about exhibiting, e-mail Edwina.Kulego@ubm.com. If you are interested in attending, visit http://www.iff-magic.com."

Visit http://www.ubmfashion.com to read more about all that
MAGIC has to offer, as well as to see a more comprehensive
calendar of the current year's trade show calendar.

12 PREPARING FOR MAGIC

Attending a fashion trade show can be amazing or the most overwhelming buying experience depending on which one you attend. For the purposes of this book we're going to focus on MAGIC, the biggest and best of all fashion trade shows.

My first MAGIC trip was just as I described it above; definitely overwhelming, but super amazing! I learned so much valuable information about buying and also all aspects of operating a successful boutique.

MAGIC is described as "the preeminent trade event in the international fashion industry, hosting global buyers and sellers of men's, women's and children's apparel, footwear, accessories and sourcing resources." This trade show takes place twice a year (February and August) in Las Vegas.

If you can attend a fashion trade show in a city near you I'd definitely encourage you to do so, but if you had to choose between all of the trade shows occurring each year, MAGIC would be the one to attend.

13 ATTENDING MAGIC:
MY EXPERIENCE

So, let me tell you about my MAGIC experience. After my first trip, I returned home and realized I'd done more learning than shopping. There was a long list of seminars with topics including, *"How to Compete with Amazon," "Buyers and Consumers Have Changed: How to Launch a Successful Brand in 2018," "Captivating & Marketing to the Millennial Customer," "E-Commerce Sins: 7 Common Mistakes That Are Hurting Your Online Business,"* and a host of other topics. My issue was that I wanted to attend all of them, but didn't have enough time to do that.

It wasn't until my last day there that I realized most of the seminars were held twice and I could have attended them at a later time. So, don't be like me. Look at the full schedule, decide which seminars you want to attend and when you want to attend them.

Ok, see how I just got distracted there!? We're supposed to be talking about buying and here I am telling you to attend seminars... But seriously, you should definitely attend them!

To be completely honest, attending MAGIC is an experience like no other. This trade show allows you to shop tons of vendors all in the same place at the same time. Whether you're looking for women's, men's, children's... whatever your heart desires you can find it at MAGIC.

Besides the seminars, another one of my favorite aspects of MAGIC was being able to place pre-orders. A pre-order is an order that you place before an item is actually available. Essentially you're asking for first dibs on this item whenever it does arrive. The coolest part about this is that your card will not be charged until the merchandise is actually available and ready to be shipped. Some vendors won't even ask for a form of payment until the item is ready to be shipped and some will ask for payment information when the pre-order is placed but won't charge you until the item arrives. Either way, you get to start building a future collection. I loved that I was able to see items for the upcoming season and start planning my collections for months to come.

As listed above, MAGIC is divided into various other shows. Each of these shows take place between two separate convention centers; the Las Vegas Convention Center and the Mandalay Bay Convention Center. Confusion can arise if you aren't aware of what is taking place at each convention center.

During this trip I was most importantly shopping for women's clothing, specifically more affordable, yet trendy women's clothing. I was determined to find new vendors that I hadn't heard of, as well build connections. I made it my mission to talk to as many people as I could and to learn as much as I could from as many people as I could while attending MAGIC.

14 BUILDING CONNECTIONS WITH VENDORS

Although I had a list of styles I was looking for as well as a budget, I made an effort to stop anytime something interesting caught my eye. I didn't stay in the booth for long, however. I took a quick lap around the booth to see what the merchandise was like as well as paid attention to their pricing. Although I wasn't purchasing anything, I always asked a very particular list of questions which you can read below:

1. Do you have a look-book as well as a business card that I can take with me? (A look-book is a pamphlet or brochure that includes photos of some the vendors current merchandise)
2. What is your name?
3. How often do you receive new merchandise?
4. Are you on FashionGo?
5. What is your typical price range?
6. Are you located in the L.A. fashion district? (It's important to ask this because you want to be build a list of vendors to shop with when/if you visit The Fashion District.)

More than likely they will ask you questions as well, if their booth is not crowded. Some of the questions they might ask are;

1. Where is your boutique located?
2. What do you sell?
3. What is your price point?

There may be other questions asked. You never know what may come of this very short conversation. During my trip to MAGIC, I stopped at one particular booth, asked my questions, and then she asked questions back. It turned out that she was the owner of the company! She was very impressed by our boutique and our mission. We exchanged contact information and although most of their pieces were a bit out of our price range she agreed to contact me via email to let me know when items were marked down or when they got cute styles that were in our price range. (Of course I had to follow up with her when I made it back home because I'm sure she met with hundreds, if not thousands of other people, and I wanted to refresh her memory.)

Communication is key, especially in a crowded and overwhelming space like MAGIC. There are workers inside every single booth that are there to help. Tell them about your shop, what you sell, what you're looking to buy and how much you're looking to spend. Be honest if something isn't in your price range. Depending on what it is, there may be room for price negotiations.

You will make your MAGIC experience 10 times harder if you don't communicate or ask for help.

15 BUILDING CONNECTIONS WITH OTHER BOUTIQUE OWNERS

Attending MAGIC is very intimidating and can be even more intimidating when you're attending alone. Don't panic though. There's probably a thousand other women (or men) who also came alone. Now, here's the tough part. You all need to connect with one another... So, one of you is going to have to work up the courage to say "hi" first.

There are tons of opportunities for this interaction to take place. Around each convention center, there are numerous seating areas. Honestly, you'd be lucky if you didn't completely bump into at least one person at every corner that you turn and I guarantee you will definitely take a few breaks to sit down and rest your feet.

My interactions usually took place while sitting; either while waiting for a seminar to begin or on the shuttle headed to/from the convention center. Sometimes I started the conversation. Sometimes I didn't. It usually began with a very simple "hi." We would then ask each other where the other was from, and what type of business they had. This usually organically leads to further conversation.

On one of my shuttle rides to the convention center I met a super sweet older woman who told me that she had been in business for 30+ years and had three boutiques in three different cities. I was so inspired! She told me that one of her struggles was social media. She just didn't understand it. Social media is one of my favorite aspects of running a business. We switched business cards and agreed to keep in contact. I agreed to help her with her social media in exchange for advice on how she had maintained her business for 30 years.

These conversations also typically led to mention of vendors that we loved or vendors that we were looking for. Essentially, we were all helping each other out, whether knowingly or unknowingly.

Remember that MAGIC serves buyers from all over the world! I guarantee that there are multiple people there that you can learn something from and multiple people that you can share knowledge with. You're bound to make some great connections at MAGIC, but you'll have to speak up in order to make the connection happen.

Every single interaction you have at MAGIC will be beneficial. Whether short or long, whether a buying experience, a seminar or a short conversation with a complete stranger, everything will be valuable to you and your boutique's success.

OK, so let's sum this up. Remember, you definitely need to have a plan when you attend MAGIC.

1. You need to know what you want to buy.

2. You need to know how much of it you want to buy.
3. You need to know how much you want to spend.
4. You need to know what vendors you're looking for.
5. You need to ask questions.
6. You need to be honest and mention your price range and what you're looking for.
7. You need to attend seminars.
8. You need to collect look-books and business cards from every single vendor booth you visit.
9. You need to meet new people and hold conversations with them.
10. You need to keep a record of what you've purchased and when it's arriving.

16 THIS IS JUST THE BEGINNING

So, there you have it! I just shared three different ways that you can find and buy merchandise for your boutique. Whether you are a new boutique owner or an experienced boutique owner, either of these options will work for you. Because I have used all three of these methods I can definitely say they are all reliable ways to buy merchandise for your boutique.

If you haven't started your boutique yet, or you are just getting ready to dive into buying, I highly recommend that you do your research and decide what exactly you want to sell and how much you want to sell it for before you purchase anything. There is a lot to choose from out there, so take the necessary steps to make the smartest buying decisions.

Buying for your boutique will most definitely come with trial and error. You will definitely purchase things and wish that you hadn't or regret paying as much for an item as you did. But, buying is definitely a process and it gets easier with time.

I hope that this book has provided you with insight and encouraged you to continue on your journey to either become a boutique owner or become a better boutique owner.

I promise, if you remember to always create a plan of action you will not fail. Remember, "if you fail to plan then you plan to fail."

Do yourself a favor and figure out exactly what you want to offer in your boutique before you spend a dime on any merchandise. If you plan accordingly, you will not fail.

This may be the end of this book, but this is just the beginning of the success that is to come.

ABOUT THE AUTHOR

Jance Chartae is a 28-year-old retail professional with almost 12 years of retail management and customer service experience.

She has worked for countless retailers such as DKNY, Michael Kors and Saks Fifth Avenue to name a few. Having held various positions ranging from sales consultant, stylist, visual merchandising manager, assistant store manager, and store manager, Jance gained an unimaginable amount of knowledge about retail and providing customer service in various environments.

Currently she manages a small boutique and resale shop in St. Louis, MO. Her current position has been an absolute door-opener for. Not only does she manage the operation of the shop, she is also the head salesperson, the social media manager, the inventory manager, the visual merchandising manager, and her favorite role, the buyer.

During her tenure in this role she has exemplified skills that she never knew she possessed. She has gratefully been allowed to run a business, essentially on her own, without the financial risk being her own.

Jance believes that many more people would be capable of finding success if more people were willing to share the knowledge that they possess with others.

So, she is now on a mission to share as much knowledge as possible with other people hoping to one day open a boutique, or currently looking to elevate their boutique business.

This book is just the first of many books to come. Jance hopes to answer as many questions and provide as much insight as she possibly can. Shoot her an email some time if you have any questions that you would like answered. You can reach her at jance@jancechartae.com.

21906588R00034

Made in the USA
Lexington, KY
12 December 2018